Opossum Opposites

For my passel, Ulysse and Azélie,

with infinite gratitude to Fab

& everyone who helped bring this book to life.

Printed in the United States of America

First Printing, 2020

ISBN-13: 978-1-7345424-0-0 Paperback
ISBN-13: 978-1-7345424-6-2 Hardcover
ISBN-13: 978-1-7345424-3-1 eBook

MOONFLOWER
press

Moonflower Press LLC
Atlanta, Georgia

For permission requests, contact Moonflower Press
at www.moonflowerpress.com

Opossum
Opposites

Written by Gina Gallois
Illustrated by Aleksandra Bobrek

Opossum babies, called joeys,
grow **big** but are born so **small**.
Each the size of a sweet pea,
Mama's pouch holds thirteen in all.

Did you know?

Opossums are **marsupials**, a type of mammal with a pouch on their belly. Opossum joeys are born after only about 13 days of development in their mother's womb. Then they crawl to her pouch to nurse and stay warm as they grow.

Newborn joeys, so soft and pink,
are **bald** with their eyes shut tight.
Growing opossums get very **furry**,
to their mama's great delight.

Did you know?

Opossum joeys are called **pinkies** for the first two
to three weeks of life until they begin to change
color and grow fur. Joeys open their eyes when
they are eight to ten weeks old.

Opossum fur may be light or dark,
though most wear a coat of grey,
with large **black** eyes, a long **white** face
and a tail the color of clay.

Opossum talk

Do opossums look like any other animals
you have seen?

Opossums have long, smooth tails that grip
by looping and curling around.
Unique tails help them climb **up**, **up**, **up**,
and keep them from tumbling **down**.

Did you know?

Opossums use their **prehensile tails** to carry
things like leaves for building nests. Their tails
also help them climb and catch themselves when
they start to fall. Joeys may occasionally hang
upside down from their tails, but as they grow,
they lose this ability.

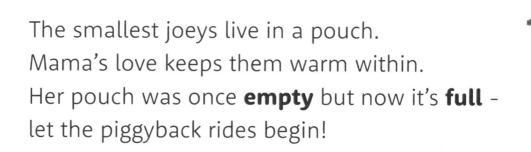

The smallest joeys live in a pouch.
Mama's love keeps them warm within.
Her pouch was once **empty** but now it's **full** –
let the piggyback rides begin!

Did you know?

A mother opossum's **pouch** is like a furry little pocket in her belly. She can care for up to 13 babies in her pouch, where they drink her milk. When joeys get too big to stay in the pouch, they ride on their mama's back, holding on tightly to her fur with their long fingers.

Opossum talk

Does your mother have a pouch? How many kids do you think she can carry on her back?

Opossums are nocturnal.
You won't see them out at noon.
They sleep all **day** while you're awake
and come out at **night** with the moon.

Did you know?

Animals who sleep during the day and go out at
night to find food are **nocturnal**. Bats, owls, and
raccoons are also nocturnal. Occasionally, it is
possible to see a mother opossum looking for food
to feed her hungry babies during the day.

Opossum talk

Are you nocturnal? What about your parents?

Feeding her babies is Mama's job.
It takes hard **work**, you know,
to satisfy her joeys' hunger
so they can **play** and grow.

Did you know?

Opossum moms carry their babies everywhere until
they no longer need to nurse when they are three to four
months old. Then the young opossums go off on their
own. Opossums are solitary creatures.

Opossums don't eat in restaurants.
They're nature's cleaner-uppers.
What's **trash** to us is **treasure** for them -
our scraps become their suppers!

Did you know?

Opossums are not picky. They are **omnivores**,
which means they eat plants and animals. They
love overripe fruit and berries as well as ticks, insects,
worms, mice, snakes, and the remains of dead animals,
also called carrion. Nothing goes to waste in nature!

Opossum talk

Are you a picky eater?

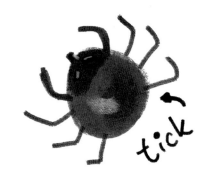

tick

Some people think opossums carry germs that make us **sick**. In fact, they keep us **healthy** because they love eating ticks.

Did you know?

Ticks are arachnids, like spiders. They feed on the blood of humans and animals. Deer ticks carry Lyme disease, a very serious illness. One opossum can eat up to 5,000 ticks each year, reducing the number of ticks that could spread the disease.

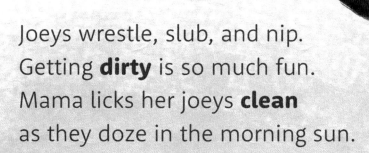

Joeys wrestle, slub, and nip.
Getting **dirty** is so much fun.
Mama licks her joeys **clean**
as they doze in the morning sun.

Did you know?

Opossums have scent memory to help them remember safe places, good paths to take and where they find food. **Slubbing**, or slobber-rubbing, is when opossums rub their heads back and forth on something they like.

Opossum talk

Do you have scent memory?
What smells make you feel safe?

Opossums may look **scary**,
with fangs and jaws open wide.
They're really just **afraid** of YOU,
so they freeze instead of hide.

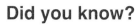

Did you know?

Opossums are gentle creatures. They
defend themselves by showing their teeth
and drooling, but they rarely bite. When
cornered, they may faint from fear and
stress so predators will leave them alone.

Opossums "play **dead**" in a pinch
when they meet a frightening stranger.
Drama gives them their best chance
to stay **alive** through the danger.

Did you know?

Opossums don't really pretend to be dead. Fainting is
an involuntary response that helps them survive. Their
heart and breathing slow down. They drool and give
off a bad smell to tell predators they would not make a
good meal. They can stay this way for up to four hours.

Opossum talk

How do you react when you are afraid?

When startled, opossums **stop** still,
frozen stiff, afraid to run.
They'll **go** once the danger passes.
Being frightened is no fun!

Did you know?

When frightened, opossums may stop in place, refusing
to move until they feel safe. You can help by bringing
dogs inside and leaving them alone until they feel safe
enough to run away.

Opossum talk

How long can you stay perfectly
still without moving - not even a whisker?

frozen with fear

Snuggled deep in Mama's pouch,
joeys travel in **safety**.
Cars will always be a **danger**,
but Mama protects her babies bravely.

You can be a helper

If you find a wounded opossum, ask an adult for help. Remember, a female could have babies in her pouch who may need special care to survive.

You can also help by telling your friends all the amazing things you know about opossums and why we should protect them.

When they see unfamiliar sights,
opossums appear to **hiss**.
Strangers are afraid of bites
but Mama gets a **kiss**.

Did you know?

The truth is, opossums look like they are hissing,
but the sound they make is more like a low growl.
Joeys make a chirping sound and mothers click
to communicate with them.

Dogs, cats, and fish make excellent **pets** –
a best friend for every child.
Opossums are cute, but please don't forget,
they're much better off in the **wild**.

Did you know?

Wildlife rehabilitators have special training so they can
take care of sick and injured wild animals. Their goal is
to release healthy animals back into their
natural habitat.

Did you know?

The Virginia opossum is the only species of marsupial native to the United States and Canada. Many other marsupials live in Mexico, South America, and Australia, too.

Possums and opossums are both marsupials, but they are actually different animals. Possums live in places like Australia and Indonesia. In everyday life, the terms possum and opossum are often used interchangeably.

Mother opossums have 12 teats, like nipples, arranged in a circle and one more in the middle for a total of 13. Opossum mothers can have up to three litters each year. That's a lot of babies!

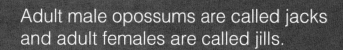

Adult male opossums are called jacks and adult females are called jills.

Opossums' low body temperature means they are mostly immune to rabies, a dangerous disease transmitted through animal bites.

Opossums are immune to snake venom and help keep venomous snake populations in check.

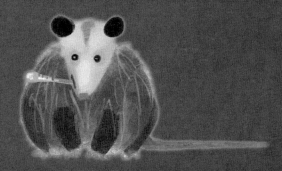

For emergency help finding a qualified wildlife rehabilitator, go to The Opossum Society website or Opossum Hotline on Facebook.

Now available from Moonflower Press...

Mama Opossum's Misadventures

written by Gina Gallois
illustrated by Aleksandra Bobrek

Will you help Mama Opossum?

Mama Opossum needs a friend to help her find
all 10 of her lost babies before morning.
There's no time to lose.
Let's find the joeys!

About the Author

Gina Gallois is a writer and opossum enthusiast turned children's book author. In a previous life, she was a French professor. She lives in Atlanta, Georgia with her husband and their two children.

When she's not writing, Gina enjoys reading with her kids, listening to audiobooks about magical places, watching her garden grow, and travelling the world. Coffee and Earl Grey tea with way too much half & half are her favorite beverages, followed closely by fizzy water.

**Please visit MoonflowerPress.com
to see what's coming next!**

Made in the USA
Coppell, TX
28 September 2020